YOUR KNOWLEDGE HAS VALUE

Bibliographic information published by the German National Library:

The German National Library lists this publication in the National Bibliography; detailed bibliographic data are available on the Internet at http://dnb.dnb.de .

Imprint:

Copyright © 2017 GRIN Verlag, Open Publishing GmbH
Print and binding: Books on Demand GmbH, Norderstedt Germany
ISBN: 9783668475359

This book at GRIN:

http://www.grin.com/en/e-book/370192/dick-and-jane-primer-in-toni-morrison-s-the-bluest-eye-as-an-aesthetic

Shaimaa Radhi

"Dick-and-Jane Primer" in Toni Morrison's "The Bluest Eye" as an Aesthetic Device

GRIN Publishing

GRIN - Your knowledge has value

Since its foundation in 1998, GRIN has specialized in publishing academic texts by students, college teachers and other academics as e-book and printed book. The website www.grin.com is an ideal platform for presenting term papers, final papers, scientific essays, dissertations and specialist books.

Visit us on the internet:

http://www.grin.com/

http://www.facebook.com/grincom

http://www.twitter.com/grin_com

Dick & Jane Primer in Toni Morrison's

"The Bluest Eye" as an Aesthetic Device

By

Assist. Lect. Shaimaa Hadi Radhi

Thi-Qar Directorate of Education

Nassiriyah / Iraq

Abstract

The focus of this paper is the narrative mechanism of employing a paragraph of "Dick and Jane" Reader which was popular in children schools in 1940s in the American United States. It educates children how to read and they hear it from the very beginning of their lives. Through such an educational system, the white dominant culture exerts its authority in oppressing black people. In her novel "The Bluest Eye", the African-American writer Toni Morrison cuts an expert of "Dick and Jane" narrative and uses it as a prologue. She repeats the paragraph three times which are highly different from each other, then dismembers it into pieces that appear as headings to some chapters of the novel. The study reveals the aesthetic purpose beyond such reproducing and dismembering of "Dick and Jane" narrative. Morrison sends a message of moral content to blacks as well as whites: On the one hand, blacks, particularly those who immersed in the white ideology, have to wake up and realize the value of their culture, heritage and language in protecting their black identity. On the other hand, whites should respect and admit the cultural and humane existence of the other and realize the merit of the black culture.

Key words: Toni Morrison, primer, "The Bluest Eye", jazz, improvisation, Call and response.

1. Introduction: Biographical and Literary Background

Morrison, who is a well-known African- American writer, was born in Lorain, Ohio. She has highly contributed to the awareness of African American literature. In her town, she was raised in a tight knit black community. Morrison's family, who migrated from the black south to the black north, watered her self-esteem and cultural identity. She grew up soaked in the African American music from spiritual and work song to blues and jazz. Her father was racist because he tasted bitterness of racism, so he despised whites and her mother told her folktales and stories; sang both jazz and opera, also her grandfather was fond in playing the violin. In this case, all" black lore, black music , black language and all the myths and rituals of black culture were prominent elements in the early life of Morrison" (McKay,1983:139). She loved storytelling and became very keen to portray black communities in her novels. Her "project of writing is outside the white gaze..., she credited the complexity and originality of African American life"(Bowers, 2010:38).

The matter of identity became central for African American writers because their culture was disrooted during slavery; they lost whatever characteristic of identity. So they determined to reclaim their identity through art. In this regard, Neal argues that " the black art is the aesthetic and spiritual sister to the black power... the black art and the black power concept both relate broadly to the Americans' desire for self-determination and nationhood"(1968:38). As an African American writer, Morrison is influenced, to a great extent, by the "major characteristics of Black art" and employs them in her fiction (Morrison, 1984:199). She is interested in the survival of black community, and instead of defining itself in relation to external ideology or the dominant group or the dominant group, it should emphasize its own past, and its own forms (Bjork, 1992:14). She aims to write novels in black language without paying attention to explain her world to white people. Her narrative language is free of oppressive norms of white culture. To use Kohler's words, she" does not allow African American tradition to be forgotten"(2006:44). Language is the mark of existence and continuity of a nation, it should be independent. According to Morrison," language is the thing that black people love so much... it's a love, passion... the worst of all possible things that could happen would be to lose that language" (Interview by Thomas Leclair,1981:4). Morrison violates the old form of writing, and "recreates something... that defines what makes a book ' black'" (McKay, 1983:421).

Generally, Morrison's work is bearable of different interpretations since she does not spoon-feed meaning to the readers. Gates (quoted in Bloom, 2010:27) describes Morrison's" writing on the one hand as popular (accessible to the reader) and difficult (demanding a close critical attention)". She is interested in making the reader indulged in rereading her work to catch the message. Her novels "refuse to tell us overtly what they mean" (Smith, 2010:10). Morrison is very keen to make readers participate, experience and create through writing process. To her, "readers and writers both struggle to interpret,... within a common language, sharable imaginative world" (Morrison,1992:xii).

Once, she describes her work comparing it to a crystal" with its different faces and layers revealing an idea from different angles and points of view" (Silver Blatt quoted in Stein, 2009:6).

One of Morrison best-known novels is "The Bluest Eye", that is published in 1970. It takes place in Morrison's home-town Lorain, Ohio in 1940-1941. It tells the tragic story of a young girl, Pecola Breedlove, who longs to have blue eyes because she sees herself ugly and is not loved by her family and community. She" wanted to rise up out of her blackness and see the world with blue eyes" (Morrison, 2007: 179). According to the dominant culture, she does not emulate ideals of beauty and worth. Such a world leads her to lose her self-esteem. She spent her time running to catch white ideals of beauty, but who can catch smoke. At the very beginning of this novel, there is a passage taken from "Dick and Jane" reader appears as prologue. What attracted me as a reader is the way in which this excerpted passage written in different ways, then this long piece is fragmented into parts that introduced some chapters of the novel as epigraphs. Here, this paper deals with this point as a central topic of the study.

2.   The Primer

"Dick and Jane" reader was so familiar in the public schools of children at the 1940s. Ahlawat acknowledges that" it privileges whiteness" (2013:56). It is a racist discourse. It represents an idealized white middle class family. Learning to read and write through it will be dangerous for black children because they will be exposed to the white values that destroy their self-esteem and identity) Gibson, 1987:160). This piece of the narrative" Dick and Jane" is very important in form and content since" it offers an interpretative key to Morrison's text", to borrow Sakaguchi's words (1996:36). Its existence prefacing the novel denotes that it is told from a child perspective. The primer is the mirror of the largest story, which is how children learn to interpret their world. Donald Gibson (1993:36) points out that the quoted phrases of the primer introduce what is to follow, offer evidence to comment upon and support the thematic implications of the main text, they inform the main text, its course, its implications within every aspect of plot, character and description. According to Klotman, " it serves as a synopsis of the tale that is to follow"(1979:123). Morrison is very deft in employing the primer as she makes it a masterpiece by itself. She goes on making changes on it to authenticate her text as African American. The changes, she made, rise many probable interpretations.

2.1. Facet One: Representations of "Dick and Jane" Narrative: Ideals, Mimics and Cast offs

I - Ideals (Stereotypes)

Here is the house. It is green and white. It has a red door. It is very pretty. Here is the family. Mother, father, Dick and Jane live in the green and white house. They are very happy. See Jane. She has a red dress. She wants to play. Who will play with Jane? See the cat. It goes meow-meow. Come and play. Come play with Jane. The kitten will not play. See Mother. Mother is very nice. Mother will you play with Jane? Mother laughs. Laugh, mother laugh. See Father. He is big and strong. Father will you play with Jane? Father is smiling. Smile, Father, smile. See the dog run. Run, dog, run. Look, look. Here comes a friend. The friend will play with Jane. They will play a good game. Play, Jane, play. (Morrison, 2007:3).

Morrison quotes directly the above paragraph of "Dick and Jane" narrative. It is an authentic replica that represents an ideal white family of middle class, although the race of Dick and Jane is not clear. Klotman (1979:123) claims that the first version symbolizes the lifestyle of the alien white world represented by the Fisher family that effects on the lives of the black children and their families while excluding them. According to this text, the white family is associated with morality, prosperity. There is no wrong with such a family, everything is perfect. Critics have called it as the "idyllic" Dick and Jane" Utopia" (Bump,2010:155). In this perfect world, there is no room to blacks, whoever than whites is hyphenated. The white culture imposes its standards of beauty as a privilege. Superiority is related to whiteness, and inferiority to blackness. Here, the decisive scale is that of colour

7

which means that the white is beautiful and the black is ugly. In this way, Africans' sense of community life is destroyed. After careful reading to the quoted text, you can find what you assume to be perfect world is just a fake, i.e you find an American family where mother, father, Dick and Jane live happily, but at the same time, Jane is alone. No member of this happy family answers her need and play with her. Then, then the white culture is just a veneer without essence.

II - Mimics or Mixed Race

This time, the quoted paragraph looks with different appearance. It shows no capitalization and punctuation; to some extent, it looks confused:

Here is the house it is green and white it has a red door it is very pretty here is the family mother father dick and jane live in the green and white house they are very happy see jane has a red dress she wants to play who will play with jane see the cat it goes meow-meow come and play with jane the kitten will not play see mother mother is very nice mother will you play with jane mother laughs laugh see father he is big and strong father will you play with jane father is smiling smile father smile see the dog bowwow goes the dog do you want to play with jane see the dog run run dog run look look here comes a friend the friend will play with jane they will play a good play jane play (Morrison, 2007:4).

The pressure of the dominant community which imposes its standards of living and physical beauty on the black community creats longing on the part of some of its members to emulate or match the standards of the stereotypes. Those members are either mimics or those who are generated by intermingling of white race with blacks (mixed race). In

8

favour of white supremacy, mimics and mixed race indulged in the customs and values of the dominant culture in order to establish an identity and win acceptance among the white society. In doing that, it seems that they are divorced from their own race. That means more prestige could be attained among the black community and privilege of better communication with the white society (Anderson, 2000:57). Within the novel the prototype characters that represent this class are Mrs. Geraldine as mimic and Maureen Peal as mixed race. They aspire to become like the white community. They " are typical mulattos who live by the white middle- class values" (Joodaki and Vajdi,2013:181). For instance, Mrs. Geraldine teaches her family the difference between coloured and black. She does her best to" get rid off the funkiness" (Morrison, 2007: 83). For her, Pecola represents everything she despises. She thinks Pecola has" all the negative features [like ugliness, poverty, disorder and filthy] of her views of black girls" (Brook, 2000:37). She always calls her" nasty little black bitch" (Morrison, 2007: 93). A character that represents the mixed race is Maureen Peal; she is a light-skinned girl with green eyes and long brown hair. She stands for a rich black family. It is light- skinned African- American family. It also despises black people. Maureen enchanted everyone at school and everywhere in her community. Like others, she thinks that she is beautiful:" I am cute!", [and Pecola is ugly] And you ugly! Black and ugly black e mos."(Ibid: 73). Then, what makes Maureen thinks that she is cute?" It is the ideology of whiteness that makes Maureen appear beautiful"(Munafo, 1995: 8).

In fact, such people are lost; they cannot be defined as white or black because" they would lose their physical markers" (Chesnutt, 2002: 845). On the other hand, white people would no longer be superior and distinctive, they" would lose their pure white race" (Ibid).

III - Cast offs

Now the quoted text is re-produced very differently for the third time. This time, it is a distorted version. There are no punctuation and capitalization; letters run together and there is no space between the words:

Hereisthehouseitisgreenandwhiteithasareddooritisverypretty

hereisthefamilymotherfatherdickandjaneliveinthegreenandw

hitehousetheyareveryhappyseejaneshehasareddressshewants

toplaywhowillplaywithjaneseethecatitgoesmeowmeowcomea

ndplaycomeplaywithjanethekittenwillnotplayseemothermoth

erisverynicemotherwillyouplaywithjanemotherlaughlaughm

otherlaughseefatherheisbigandstrongfatherwillyouplaywithja

nefatherissmilingsmilefathersmileseethedogbowwowgoesthe

dogyouwanttoplaydoyouwanttoplaywithjaneseethedogrunrun

dogrunlooklookherecomeafriendwillplaywithjanetheywillplaya

goodgameplayjaneplay(Morrison,2007:4).

This version symbolizes the darker-skinned black people who are under segregation and suffering of oppression practiced by the white ideology of beauty and prosperity. Within the novel, such circumstances correspond to the life of black families like the MacTeers and Breedlove. For example, the MacTeers are aware of the danger of submission to the white ideology. They can challenge the oppression but the victims of such oppression lack this challenge and awareness (Grewal, 1998:21). The mother, Mrs MacTeer feeds her daughters, Claudia and Frieda, black cultural values. Claudia and Frieda do not care about their blackness, but they are very pleased with:" we felt comfortable in our skin... "(Morrison.2007:74). They blame members of their community who foster their oppressors' values and white standard of beauty. On the other hand, the Breedloves try to align themselves with their oppressors. For example, Pecola's mother Mrs Breedlove, who works for a white family, does not care about her daughter, and she teaches her nothing positive. Moreover, she sometimes becomes very furious at her daughter. Once, when Pecola dropped a pie juice on the floor, she abused her with an assault saying: "Crazy fool... my floor, mess...look what you... work...get on out...now that.. crazy... my floor, my floor" (Ibid:109). As a result, Pecola is abandoned and defeated by her family as well as community. Then , she starts her dreaming journey to be acceptable by having beautiful blue eyes which are the scale of beauty. She thought if her eyes were different, others would say:" why, look at pretty-eyed Pecola. We mustn't do bad things in front of those pretty eyes" (Ibid: 46). It is the beginning of her insanity.

2.2   Facet Two: The Third pastiche: an Urge of Unity (Collectivity)

Hereisthehouseitisgreenandwhiteithasareddooritisverypretty

hereisthefamilymotherfatherdickandjaneliveinthegreenandw

hitehousetheyareveruhappyseejaneshehasaredressshewants

toplaywhowillplaywithjaneseethecatitgoesmeowmeowcomea

ndplaycomeplay...(Morrison,2007:4).

These fused letters may represent black individuals who migrated to Harlem which is: the Mecca of black people in 1920" according to Tally (2007:34) to make their voice heard and existence acknowledged. Harlem is the centre of African Americans (artiste, writers, poets, singers) who migrated from the South to the North to live in a united black community. Culture pressure forces African Americans in general to migrate, and their" migration [...] reflected a calculation of unfamiliar but enticing opportunity weighed against the realities of the jim south" (Wiese. 2009:40).

In the north, they fused in their own distinctive community to make their own identity. In her narrative writing, Morrison tries to highlight the village or tribal quality of living by which the blacks join together to get their survival. Concerning this, Morrison declares that she writes what she calls" village literature", which is written for the village or tribe of the black people(La Clair,1981:2). In this way, African Americans' journeys took the form of kith networks, which are widespread suburban living patterns. [And] by so doing, they challenged and

12

subverted a central element of the dominant suburban ethos which was white supremacy"(Wiese,2009:144).

Morrison has made these black letters jumbled and centric in order to attract the reader's interest. She highlights the significance of resorting to collectivity or unity as a style of living for blacks to keep their identity and minimize the social distance that white maintains as privilege. Morrison presents such a situation of empathy in her novel as she makes MacTeers take Pecola who has been despised and refused by by her community. MacTeers's home was the only shelter for her. Claudia and Frieda assured that: Frieda and I stopped fighting each other and concentrated on our guest, trying to keep her from feeling outdoors...She laughed when I clowned for her, and smiled and accepted gracefully the food gifts my sister gave her" (Morrison, 2007;18-19).

2.3   Facet Three: Equal Function: Dismembering of Dick & Jane Primer & that of the White Doll as an aesthetic Function

As has been mentioned before, Morrison aesthetically dismembered the passage of Dick and Jane primer into parts making them isolated house, mother, father, cat, dog and friend. Such an aesthetic action by Morrison is to function as a textual subversion or violence. Also, it made the ideal text lose its effect as an ideal cultural text. The writer offers us another case by which we can find that the main character Claudia, who acts as the spokeswoman of the black community, expresses her hatred of the child star and all the white icons like the blue-eyed doll. She dislikes the white ideals and respects her aesthetic blackness. She always wonders why whiteness is associated with beauty. In an attempt to find an answer, she begins dismembering the white doll to pieces:

"I had only one desire to dismember it to find the beauty, the desirability that had escaped me... I fingered the face, ... Break off the tiny fingers, bend the flat feet, loosen the hair, twist the head around, and the thing made one sound..."(Morrison,2007: 20-21).

Here, Morrison challenges" the superiority of white culture" 9Shahabi and Asghar Emami Pour, 2012: 288) by focusing on the aesthetic reaction of her black narrative protagonist against the humiliating actions practiced by the white oppressors. Such an aesthetic action of dismembering represents textual violence done by the black against real violence done by the whites. The narrator Claudia assures that: " I learned how repulsive this disinterested violence was, that it was repulsive because it was disinterested, my shame floundered about for refuge"(Morrison,2007:23). In this case, both actions are violent reaction against more violent community. Peach (2000:38) argues that the dismembering of the white doll by Claudia is very analogous to Dick and Jane mythology.

2.4   Facet Four: Musicality of "Dick and Jane" Primer

Generally speaking, the black music has a healing effect. For African Americans, it is their artistic expression which frames an aesthetic device of reference for black authors. According to Morrison, ' black music is thus a counter expression, an alternative to the ways of western expressive forms" (Softing, 1995:82). From this perspective aspect, Morrison tries her best to make her writing black jazz-like because jazz music provided" a sense of power and control, a sense of meaning and direction, in a world that often seems anarchic"(Lawrence, 1998:440).

Morrison's writing is rich in musical strategies that makes it very effective. She" writes through the analogy, even through an imitation of music"(Rigney, 1999:8). She wants her narrative language to do " what music used to do" for people in America(Mckay, 1983:160). In so doing, she aesthetically tries to keep a unique culture of her oppressed and humiliated people.

As it is already mentioned," the primer is an interpretative key to Morrison's novel"(Sakaguch, 1996:36). Therefore, what is applied of technique in the text can be applied to the quotation of "Dick and Jane" primer. For example, Morrison dismembers the primer into parts as headers to some chapters where the components of the white family: house, mother, father, dog, cat and friend are isolated. Such an aesthetic strategy by her is like what the jazz musician does. According to Shahabi and Asghar Emami Pour (2012:289)" the improvisatory aspect of the primer, which acts as the epigraph to the chapters of the novel, gives it a jazz –like quality". Another aspect is that" Dick and Jane" primer is narrated by the third- person narrative voice and this is like the jazz musician's art. For black musicians, jazz is a kind of disobedience to tradition. Jazz musicians are not constrained in what they do by the usual conventions of the musical community, and like this is Morrison, she is not guided but free of constrains of white language. Aesthetically, she employs this feature of jazz in her work. Here" jazz improvisation is story telling" (Bjerstedt, 2014:305). Morrison brings disorder to ordered structure. To her, " both music and literature bring change, originality and unpredictability to an already recognized and established structure(Berre,2008:82).

The third feature, which makes the quoted piece of primer looks like a piece of jazz music is "call and response" style. Such a style is originally developed among slaves, where the caller begins a story and the listening community respond (Mutere,2005 cited in Kohler, 2006: 45). It is really an aesthetic oral African expression. To borrow Smitherman's words, Call – and – response is:

" an African communication process of spontaneous verbal and non-verbal interaction between speaker and listener in which all of the speaker's statements" calls" are punctuated by expressions" responses" from the listener" (1985: 104).

Like the speaker or musician, the writer calls his improvised message and the reader responds to this message aesthetically. Morrison in her article" The Reader as Artist" states that" the words on the page are only half the story, the rest is what you bring to the party" (quoted in Collins, 2010:30). She leaves an aesthetic room for the reader to experience, create, participate and enter the story. In this respect, she says that her" writing expects, demands participatory reading. It's not just about telling the story, it's about involving the reader..." (Tate, 1985:125). She wants the reader to take part emotionally or politically and not to be an observer only. Such a participation, on the part of the reader, is going to be an aesthetic message that could be transmitted throughout a black feminist narrative discourse.

3.   Conclusion

The primer" Dick and Jane" is highly important in function and form. Such a text in its different citations at the beginning of the novel has the techniques and strategies that the novel itself has. It is the real story that causes the textual story to be told. Morrison has dressed it all her narrative techniques that are extremely black. The different representations of the primer quoted: classes of community, oral traditions of blacks: jazz music, call-and-response, collectivity of black community, all make the text to look black not white. Aesthetically, she shows a distinctive black language that represents the counter expression to the white one. It is Morrison's aesthetic goal to make her writing black out of the white gaze. Here, her work is an experimental and improvisatory. She directs an aesthetic message to whoever white or black that" black is beautiful", black is centric not ex-centric. Through art, Morrison proves black identity, existence and power. As one of the most significant African American writers, she declared her responsibility as an aesthetic healer to reclaim black identities stating that" the job of recovery is ours"(Davis, 1986:413). She tries to throw a rope of awareness to blacks who are drowning in the sick values of the dominant oppressive culture.

References

Ahlawat, A. (2013)." Eco-Feminist Study of Toni Morrison's Novels: The Bluest Eye, Sula and Beloved". In International Journal of Humanities and Social Science Invention. Vol.2, Issue81, pp.56-58.

Anderson, E. (2007)" African American Class Structure. The Emerging Philadelphia". In Annals of the American Academy of Political and Social Science (2000), 5.68, pp.54-76.

Berre, T. (2008) Variations on a Theme: The Role of Music in Toni Morrison's Jazz. Tromsφ University.

Bjerstedt, S. (2014) Story Telling in Jazz Improvisation: Implications of a Rich Intermedial Metaphor. Sweden: Lund University.

Bjork, B.P. (1992) The Novel of Toni Morrison. New York: Peter Lang.

Bloom, H. (ed.) (2010) Toni Morrison's The Bluest Eye: Bloom's Guides: Comprehensive Research and Study Guides. New York: Infobase Publishing.

Bowers, R., S. (2010). "A Context for Understanding Morrison's Work". In Critical Insights: Toni Morrison (2012). Salem Press. Retrieved from salem press.com/ store/pdfs/Morrison-critical-insights.pdf.

Brooks, J. B. (2000) Quit as it's kept: Shame, Trauma and Race in the Novels of Toni Morrison. Albany: State University of New York Press.

Bump, J. (2010) " Racism and Appearance in The Bluest Eye: A Template for an Ethical Emotive Criticism". In College Literature. Vol.37, No.2 (2010). West Chester University, pp.147-170.

Chesnutt, W. C. (2002) " The Future American" . In Warner Sollers (ed.) Charles W. Chesnutt's Stories, Novels and essays. New York: The Library of America, pp.845-863.

Collins, J. (2010) Bring on the Books for Everyday: How Literary Culture Became Popular Culture. Duke University Press.

Davis, C. (1986) "Interview with Toni Morrison". In Danielle Taylor-Guthrie (1994) Conversation with Toni Morrison. Jackson: University Press of Mississippi, pp. 412- 421

Gibson, D. (1987)" Text and Counter Text in The Bluest Eye". In LIT, Literature, Interpretation, Theory 1.1-2 (1989), pp. 19-32.

--------(1993)" Text and Counter Text in The Bluest Eye". In Harold Bloom (2007) Toni Morrison's The Bluest Eye: Bloom's Modern Critical Interpretations. New York: Infobase Publishing, pp. 35-53.

Grewal, G. (1998) Circles of Sorrow, Lines of Struggle: The Novels of Toni Morrison. Boston: Louisiana State University Press.

Joodaki , H. A. and Vajdi, A. (2013) " Toni Morrison's Talks of an Unhomely World; A Post Colonial Reading of The Bluest Eye: A Study Based on Homi, K. Bhabha's Theories". In International Journal of English Language and Literature Studies (2013), 2.3, pp.176- 187.

Klotman, P.R. (1979)" Dick and Jane and the Shirley Temple Sensibility in The Bluest Eye". In Black American Literature Forum.Vol.13, No.4, pp.123- 125.

Kohler, P. (2006) Realization of Black Aesthetics in Toni Morrison's The Bluest Eye. Thesis, University of Tampere.

Lawrence, W. L. (1998) "Jazz and American Culture". In Robert, G. O'Meally (ed.) The Jazz Cadence of American Culture. New York: Columbia University Press, pp.

LeClair, T. (1981) An Interview with Morrison: The Language Must Not Sweat. Retrieved from http:// new republic. com/ article/95923/ the-language-must-not-sweat.

McKay, N. (1983)" An Interview with Toni Morrison". In Danielle Taylor-Guthrie (1994) Conversation with Toni Morrison. Jackson University Press of Mississippi, pp. 138-155.

Morrison, T. (1984) "Rootedness: The Ancestors as Foundation". In Hazel Arnett Ervin (ed.) (1999) African American Literary Criticism 1773-2000. New York: Twayne Publisher, pp.198- 202.

--------(1992) Playing in the Dark: Whiteness and the Literary Imagination. Cambridge: Harvard University Press.

---------(2007) The Bluest Eye. USA: Vantage

Munafo, G. (1995)" No Sign of Life- Marble- Blue Eyes and Lake front Houses in The Bluest Eye". In LIT: Literature, Interpretation, Theory. Vol.6, No. 1-2, pp.1-19.

Neal, L. (1968)" Black Art ". In The Drama Review (1968) Vol.12, No. 4, P.38.

Peach, L. (2000) Toni Morrison. London: Macmillan.

Rigney, H. B. (1999) The Voices of Toni Morrison. USA: Ohio State University Press.

Sakaguchi, M. (1996) The Marigolds Do Not Bloom: Toni Morrison's The Bluest Eye. Retrieved from http:// hdl.hand.net? 11094.

Shahabi, H. and Asghar Emami, A. (2012). "The Impact of Langston Hughe's Poetry on Toni Morrison's The Bluest Eye: An Afro-American Critical Reading". In Iranian EFL Journal (2012). Vol.8, No. 4. Retrieved from www/ Iranian-efl-journal.com/index/2012.index.

Smitherman, G. (1985) Talki and Testifyin: The Language of Black America> Detroit. Wayne State University Press.

Smith, V. (2010) Toni Morrison: Writing the Moral Imagination. UK: West Sussex: Wiley- Black Well.

Softing, I. (1995)" Carnival and Black American Music as Counterculture in Toni Morrison's The Bluest Eye and Jazz". University of Bergen. In American Studies in Scandinavia 27 (1995), pp. 81-102.

Stein, F. K. (2009) Reading, Learning, Teaching Toni Morrison. USA: Peter Lang.

Tally, J. (2007) The Cambridge Companion to Toni Morrison. New York: Cambridge University Press.

Tate, C. (ed.) (1985) Black Women Writers at Work. New York: Continuum.

Werrlein, T, D. (2005) "Not So Fast, Dick and Jane: Reimaging Childhood and Nation in The Bluest Eye". In MELUS 30.4 (2005), pp.53-72.

Wiese, A. (2009) The Places of their Own: African American Suburbanization in the Twentieth Century. Chicago and London: The University of Chicago Press.